Faith for Today

IN SEARCH OF A NEW PERSPECTIVE

Norman Bakken, PhD

Norman K Bakken

Brush Fork Press

2018

PREFACE

The following thoughts are offered to a group of participants of wide experience and a variety of professional backgrounds who meet with a view to a fellowship in learning, open to the insights of others and eager to be informed of new and recent developments in science and philosophy. This participant is open to criticism, suggestions and insights which would contribute to the life and understanding of our contemporaries. The same applies to all those who might be given to share in the discussion.

Norman K Bakken

Norman K Bakken

Spark of life,

Where do you find it?

You catch a glimpse of it in the eyes of a playful child, responding to the smile of an old man, celebrating the vibrancy now lost but not forgotten, reenacted in life You catch a glimpse of it in the eyes of a child, responding to the energy still at work in one so small.

The child is dancing in the aisles of the library, where the mother, with loving care, seeks to open the eyes of that child to the wonders of art and stories to awaken the imagination, moving him toward a creative wondrous life.

How is it that the spark of life is so easily forgotten in the routine of adults, caught in the web of a literal and fixed view of reality.

Where do I find myself at this stage of a long and varied life? Have all hopes dissolved? Have dreams vanished? Will there be a possible carryover of the openness and expectancy of the child?

Would that I could play again in the wild expectancy of the child, uninhibited by the sceptical eyes of those whose fixed notions allow for no play. When imagination falters, possibility disappears, and the coming generation is hindered in the evolution of the renewed wonders of creation.

May I be given to continue as a child, running with glee with what is given, "forbid them not, for of such is the kingdom of heaven."

And so, I move into the painful journey with a fresh start, seeking to capture something of what might seem lost.

FAITH FROM A NEW PERSPECTIVE

INTRODUCTION

Every age in every culture has had its own way of giving expression to faith--faith in life, faith in the realities of nature, faith in others and faith in one's self-or, if you will, faith in 'God.'

How does our faith come to expression given the perspectives and convictions which shape the language and thoughts of people today? 1 am presuming, of course, that those who lay claim to faith or truth are anxious to give expression to the same in a way that will be meaningful and clear. It must convince someone whose life and work are conditioned by a world view scarcely known or understood by past generations. I would presume, of course, that we are all in agreement that we would wish to be mutually informed of language and thought pervading our culture in this time that we would hope to be recognized as informed contemporaries.

Given that language and those thoughts how could we give expression to faith in the light

3

of current perspectives? I would wish to raise the questions, remain open to the dialogue and move in a direction that will be creatively effective for promoting the unfolding of life and faith today. I do this without any presumption that what I have to say or propose is the last word. There is so much we have still to learn from one another and from the world around us.

Seeking a New Perspective. My Present Quandary

I am no longer comfortable when asked to express my faith in the words of the creeds or confessions of the Christian Church of which I am a member, trained and ordained as a pastor and professor, having served in various capacities for a period of sixty-five years. Called to serve as an instructor in Biblical Literature and Languages I was soon to become aware of the evolutionary nature of language itself so that expressions of thousands of years ago cannot be taken literally when understood in the light of the findings of modern science and thought. Our understanding of the earth's origins and of our own relationship to the elements, we need to acknowledge our complete interdependence upon those and on one another. We must remain open, flexible and resilient, if we are to survive and remain healthy along with all nature of which we are a part. Life cannot remain stagnant. So, too, our faith depends on the realities of life that are shared by everyone and everything that exists. To see ourselves as apart and independent is impossible. We are interdependent, and that interdependence demands a healthy relationship with the elements of which we consist and the wellbeing of others who, like us, are part of the human family.

These November days have seen the first signs of frost, turning the greens of summer into the many splendored colors of autumn, yellow, maroon, red and gold. Mine has been an overly abundant experience of the golden years, shared with my beloved and our family and friends. When I am tempted to regrets in the experience of aging, I must remember that my life, which is life shared with the whole of creation, will continue when the reflection that was mine is forever contained in those who follow, those things and those people. So, my constant prayer and hope is that we will together care not only for one another but for this earth of which we are but miniscule parts, utilizing its resources wisely; avoiding as much as possible its waste, and remembering that insofar as we destroy any part we contribute to the eventual destruction of our gift of life.

So, I give thanks for every other, every other thing and every other person, and I wish them Godspeed in all that they do and in all to which they aspire. They will find, as I have, that the tender graces of love, kindness, understanding, compassion and justice will accrue to the benefit of every other, connecting, compelling, and promoting all that we would hope for, a world overflowing with life that lasts for everything and everyone, in our miniscule part of the universe, our world, our earth.

So keep coming, days and nights of new beginnings, and may I once more be assured and bring that same assurance to others that the best is yet to come and that we are given the grace to be a part of the same, one name among the endless names of life that is beyond all naming, the creative spark that was there in the beginning, the element that is beyond naming, uncaptured by words of any kind, life together, one with the whole.

<u>Sense of the Sacred. The Origin of Faith.</u>

Am I mirrored? May I assume that I amount to something? Is there anything unique and of worth in this human frame in which I find myself? Subconsciously we may know there is something of the sacred within each of us. The infant has no choice in the matter. She/he simply demands attention and satisfaction for what is given. Finding ourselves numbered among others is an awareness which may be sublimated, if not entirely subdued. A part of our religious orientation may infuse a sense of the opposite—we are anything but sacred. We are "sinful and unclean." Once that recitation of self-understanding is firmly established and repeatedly emphasized the possibility of rising above that feeling may be interpreted as arrogance or denial of reality. We are trapped.

I make no bones about the fact that I am and have been responsible for some bad decisions and unworthy acts. I know of no one who would venture to deny the same. But at the base of life lies a need for understanding too often subdued by persons and institutions built to dominate and define us. Not all of that is negative. I need to be confronted by my weaknesses and failures. I need to work through my obligation to others as well as to myself. But a life that is dominated by that kind of subservience is rather limited and unhappy to say the least, and unproductive of positive results in personality development and in relation to society

A new form of awareness has come to me, gradually working away at a negative self-image and now, at an age when it may make little difference to others besides myself. I have thought that the highest form of faith was within God. Perhaps that is as it should be. But imagine my delight and release in discovering that words like "God" is misleading. 1 may also be understood to mean "God is a believer." Place that together with the claim that we are, all of us, part of the creation of God—part of the creative imagination, the creative impulse or energy of the universe (however you might put it), then I am persuaded that "God" believes in me—that there is something uniquely blessed and productively formed as part of this world in which we find ourselves.

God believes in me. And if God believes in me then I am bound to conclude that I ought to believe in myself, to say otherwise would be to lay the guilt on the origin of our beings. And if I am given to believe in the possibilities of my own life and existence then, surely, I must regard others--things and people—as part of that creative imagination of which I am a part. And if that is the case, then I must conclude that all things, and all people are in some sense sacred and to be regarded as such.

This belittled self may not be but an infinitesimal portion of what life is all about—I can and will live with that—but I am part of the whole. And so are all other things and people of which I am a part and with whom my ultimate identity rests.

In Search of a New Perspective

The Need for Continued Growth Never Ends

I am sitting in my study on the first day of the new year. The feeling of being alone is pervasive. My first love came to the end of her journey just a day short of four months ago. Our eldest daughter, Minda, died in a horrible accident, in Minneapolis, her chosen home town, in October of 2005, victim of a careless driver. Words which her niece, our granddaughter, Marija, spoke at her memorial service, come to mind. Marija is now far away in Dubai, pursuing with her betrothed, a career in law. The feeling of distance, even with many friends nearby. brings me to the remembrance of past moments which, though painful, are a part of what gave our lives meaning. I will remember Marija's words from that memorial service for Minda, embodying as they do, the legacy of our daughter, surrounded like her mother with a thousand mourners, who carry on through the love and care implanted in life. That after all, is due I hope, to having struggled to pervade the nature of my own thoughts, implanted in me from my birth to the present, by people, all kinds of people who were what for me constitutes the essence of the truly human. The Jesus I have come to know continues to be present in lives equally dedicated to self-giving love for the preservation of life which will last. That life and that love are smothered, to an extent, by the formation of prescribed creeds and hardened liturgical forms. So, then as now, the struggle for growth in understanding can be difficult to pursue and to convey to others whom we must respect and consider. So, the only course is to continue to save, not only for the building of one's own perspective, but for the broadening of the base for others on the road of life we are given to travel together.

Difficult for most of us to accept is the fact that many traditions we bring with us from the past are irrelevant to the present generation. We might liken that to the fact that much of what the present generation takes for granted as familiar and indispensable is difficult for us to assimilate. My own struggle in using the computer is an example along with the number of wireless gadgets considered essential to modern day to day living. I am finally ready to subscribe to the use of a wireless cell phone, especially when combined with the ability to transmit and receive emails and print replies. Primary grades which taught us how to read and write, are now somewhat minimized to add the dire need of learning the agility needed for the use of laptops. With age we are forced to admit our increasing lack of resilience. Dogmatic rigidity is still one of the common ailments of religious conformity, the older and the repeated use of same adds to our lack of resilience in learning new modes of thought and life or of adapting the traditional.

Children are fascinated by the introduction of new thinking. Perhaps that is what Jesus illustrated with his sayings "Blessed are the little children and forbid them not, for of such is the kingdom of heaven." Childlike fascination may perhaps awaken our aged minds to new insights and efforts in the evolving struggle for a meaningful life, a life that lasts.

A JOURNEY OF FAITH

Life is a journey. Each of us has followed a different path. All of us have so much to learn from the experiences of the others. With that in mind I would like to share with you a little about the path I have been on, hopeful that one day I may catch a glimpse of the journey that has brought you to this day.

I realize that I could never begin to share much that would be of value to you were I to reach back over the ninety years I have known. So, I have decided to seek to relate the nature of the path as it appears to me now, knowing full well that I still have much to learn. Around every curve there will be some new vista, some new understanding which eludes me at this moment.

Apart from faith there would be no life, no beginning to the journey. From the moment we are born someone must believe in us enough to provide the nurture and care we need to grow and survive. We are then dependent on the care of others, and we still are.

14

For most of my life I have been involved in the struggle for finding and growing in faith, convinced that so much depended on me, on how I thought and how I expressed my faith. Like so many in our culture we have been conditioned to assume that life for us was dependent on our acceptance of certain creeds and practices inherited from generations of the past. There is no way we can avoid that. We need to pay attention to the understandings and the misunderstandings of earlier generations. But in matters of faith and life we know that there are so many mysteries we have yet to unravel.

Little by little I have come to see that the source for a strong and vibrant faith does not depend primarily on me but is always to be found outside of myself. Faith cannot grow and survive in isolation. Its source lies beyond what we can see, touch or demonstrate in any final way. Its primary source lies beyond our personal reach. It belongs to the very nature of life as a whole. It is at the heart of the creation itself. It belongs to God.

But let me quickly add that by using such a word do not presume in any way to name, describe or grasp in whole or in part what we mean when we use the word God. We cannot name God.

I am reminded of a conversation I had with the street sweeper who was the first one up and out in the morning at our campus setting in Bangalore. I understood that his faith was derived from Hindu traditions. I said to him, "You have many gods in India, don't you?" "Oh yes," he replied, "We have many names for the unnamable One. " When I use the word God, therefore, I am pointing to the creative impulse, energy or source of everything and everyone. On that basis I cling to a tradition that has come down to us in so many ways, the tradition that tells us, "God is real."

From that I have come to realize, at least in part, God believes in me. God is the primary mover, the ultimate subject of faith--not the object. And if God believes in me then I must begin to believe in myself as part of the creative imagination of God, no matter how small or insignificant that part may be. And if that is the case, then I must also believe in others--all things and all people-- as part and parcel of the creative Imagination at work in the universe. Then, I must ask, coming out of the Christian tradition, where does Jesus come in as the marker on the road of faith and life? There is no doubt that Jesus was an exceptional and unique embodiment of what God is all about. And what he and others gave us to see is it is true of everyone and everything. All people should be given to realize they are part and parcel of what God is all about. (See the conclusion of John Steinbeck's play in story form "Burning Bright." "Every child is the child of God.")

You are unique. You are one of a kind. If I would wish to know or give expression to what God is all about then I must learn to be attentive to everything and everyone as part of the wonder of the creative imagination of God.

Faith is first a command to be attentive, to look for the sacred, the holy, the awesome wonder of life that is to be gleaned from the everyday things and people I meet.

We have all been guilty of assuming that we and we alone--Christians, Baptists, Lutherans, Catholics—know God. That reminds me of the story of Krishna, one of the most popular gods in the Hindu pantheon. He loved to dance. Once, coming to a village, he was told all the maidens were in the forest dancing. He joined them, multiplying himself so that he could dance with each one. But when one maiden thought that she, and she alone, had Krishna, he disappeared!

So, my gospel at this late stage in my life is an expression of the that God believes in us—the whole world of things and people— and we must revere the earth, love and respect one another, knowing that we are all equally a part of the process of giving birth to life—life, love and true being. We are asked to become all that God would intend us to be, singly and together. That is our mission in life.

God loves us. God believes in us. God would have us be reflections of the wonder of being, of loving, of caring and of going forward on the journey of life.

Together we are on the journey of life. Together we will be given to see more and more of the wonder of life. And together we will contribute to the ongoing life of others in this world of ours.

A Sense of the Sacred. Mystery and Silence.

Despite the vast expansion of knowledge in so many areas of scientific research, we know there is imperceptible profound depth to existing and emergent realities of which we know virtually nothing. We may be able to say with some certainty that from those depths the creative forces of life and change are still in process. There lies the mystery. There lies the time at which science remains silent. In the silence we might find room for what we might call spirituality. Any true sense of the sacred needs be attentive to the silence. The scientist and the philosopher do well to listen and find wisdom.

Might we learn from that? Might we learn to be silent? Attentive? Sensitive to the unseen, the unfathomable, the mystery yet to unfold? Could we be spared the claims of voices proclaiming a truth which purports to give voice to the transcendent, spawning pretension?

Throughout most of my life, and more especially in the pursuit of theological disciplines, tradition has been taken literally, leading to the claim that we may know with

Norman K Bakken

certainty those matters which disclose the mystery of life's origin, essence and goal. The crystallization of religious dogma too often replaced the awesome wonder which compels humility.

I find it particularly burdensome at this stage of my life to be compelled to recite ancient creeds which purport to unfold the mystery not only of God, but of the very God, the substance of God, the explanation of the origin and the intent of the unfolding events of which we are a part. Behind the most sacred of all traditions is the reminder that God is above naming, though we may speak of the "unnamable One." I was once more brought to a profound respect for that reminder by the street sweeper on the campus of United Theological College Bangalore when I said, "You have many gods in India, don't you?" To which he replied, Oh, yes, we have many names for the unnamable One. "

A Sense of the Sacred. Nature and Divinity.

Am I able to define divinity? Of course not. Would I deny the divinity of nature? By Lutherans? From the time I was a child one could not have convinced me that mother, father, brother, sister, and related family and friends were not a part of the sacred whole. Of course, there was instead in my life even from early days of childhood that some were less sacred then others! No abstract thoughts were involved, only the hints of suspicion and doubt about a difference that should divide the best of life from what is perhaps less. Only in time, regrettably over the span of many years, I would come to see that our speculation and doubts, unfounded though they may be, would allow me the view that most all of life is sacred. Any thought to the contrary would have to include a judgment upon the nature of my own life. That doubt has become dominant in society as we know it. Faith in what is given, in the nature of all things and all persons, has had a shadow of doubt cast over the whole. A judgmental attitude is prominent, a distinction created between reality and a mindset that defies reason and the essence of nature, the stuff of which we are made.

Life is sacred. The Hindu tradition a conglomerate of beliefs coming out of a vast influx of societal changes, has at its core precisely that conviction. By what other means would it be possible to accommodate strands of migrating cultural varieties that contributed to the world's second largest population? Our own traditions, both religious and scientific, are, at base, aware of the same reality. Only a speculative desire for authority and control, such as we in dogmatic hangovers of earlier times, can vie for a different attitude toward life. And that is what separates us, preventing an evolving consciousness able to make room for the creative process which may enhance awareness of our essential unity, our needed responsibility in caring for the earth and its inhabitants whoever they might be.

<u>Never Alone.</u>

Recently I picked up a book which explores the nature and function of dreams. I remember some time earlier in my life when I believed I seldom had dreams. I remember I thought the reason for that was my mind and my life were at rest and in good order and that, therefore, dreams did not disturb my consciousness. Now I discover that virtually all living organisms have dreams, not only humans, that dreams may be pointing to obstacles in the evolutionary development of our personalities, and that we should pay attention to their parabolic, metaphoric meanings, in order that a full consciousness of our present and potential development might progress.

Our children, we've discovered, have sometimes viewed their parents as somewhat narcissistic, self-centered, seeking satisfaction primarily for themselves. We have found that difficult to accept but, with more time to reflect, we have had to see that yes, we, as parents and as individuals, have been vitally concerned that what we have thought important should be of primary consideration. We assume, of course, we know what is best--for us and for others,

23

including our children. We know our children love us and wish the best for us. So, we must be attentive to the possibility that their slant on our personalities has some validity.

I am thinking of a dream I had just recently, a strange and disturbing dream, one that on the surface makes no sense at all. To my knowledge I have never been in a horse and carriage. The nearest thing to that was a boyhood remembrance of accompanying my father and a neighboring farmer who were distributing manure onto the field of our vegetable garden from the loaded wagon drawn by a workhorse out on Kellogg Marsh, the place where we had a little cottage in the early thirties, In the dream the horse was of the type you would see in a story from the 1800's depicting a country scene from England. The carriage was small, not built for passengers, meant for one or two at the most. I was the driver. I had come to a small rise on the hill when another man tried to hoist himself aboard. I obviously did not want him there. I was trying to push him away. Why would I possibly do that? I think of myself as generally fond of people, trying to serve in any way I can, so how would you explain my exclusion of someone who, it would seem, simply wished to go in the same direction?

I've tried to find a plausible interpretation. The only one I can think of may be based on the act that, recently, I had felt inhibited, stymied, restrained from exercising my knowledge and talents in my chosen field of endeavor--leadership in the church specifically, in the interpretation of Biblical traditions. I have felt hemmed in by a very conservative, if not literalistic, rendering of the stories presented in scripture and capped by creedal formulae which become abstractly metaphysical, largely out of character with Judeo-Christian precepts. So, the thought occurs to me that, perhaps, I have tried too hard to forge a path for myself, cutting myself off from close relationships with those heading in what they presume to be the same direction, a path leading to the same or similar goals. As a critic of the system, the establishment, that is an understandable inclination, and a dangerous one in that I would be hurting only myself by seeking to go my way alone. Impatience and intolerance indicate isolation and an exaggerated importance attached to myself, without sufficient regard for the situation of others. That kind of behavior is hardly fitting for anyone regardless of fields of competence and the nature of present conclusions as to meaning and direction.

No matter where we are in life we are never alone. Those who appear to intrude and interrupt us on our path have, probably, something to contribute to our understanding and to the goals we would set for ourselves and others. Perhaps our children have something more to contribute to our understanding which we, as parents, have overlooked, no matter how well intentioned our actions have been or, at least, have seemed to be for us.

In Others.

Think what the world would be like were we to look upon everyone we meet as sacred!

I have been thought of as a "romantic" when it comes to my philosophy of life. I could hardly dispute that. I do look for the impossible is many impossible ways. But I must also confess to being something of a realist, simply because I prefer to meet reality insofar as I am able, come what may. Many times, if not usually, reality would prevent me from taking the steps to do and to be what my plans and wishes would call for. But I have been amazed at the number of times when choices which seem impossible of good results served to bring about even more than I ever dreamed. I would never have made it through college or grad school had I waited for assurances based on probability both personal and financial.

Regarding others there might be all kinds of reasons for skepticism. There are people who seem, at base, obstinate, negatively disposed, ready to be everything you would dislike or disown. And I am certain I appeared to be just that kind of fellow by others. But I believe we could agree that, just as we know no two persons are alike, that each one is unique. So also, were we to look closely enough, we would find a sacred dimension to people who appear to us, at first, to be anything but that.

Just as faith is a matter of attentiveness, attentive to everything and everyone around us, with a view to guidance which can lead us on a productive path, so attentiveness is required to discern that element in others which is indispensable to the whole. We are in it together, after all. And sooner or later we will find that ignoring that unique element in the other, that part perhaps so different from what we would imagine, is an element of our own wellbeing and fulfillment. My worst enemy might prove to be my best friend in circumstances that give rise to interdependence, when we know that we need each other, especially in desperate times, and we will come together in surprising and productive ways. We need reminders of that if we are to survive and thrive.

Unknown, Denied.

Awareness of the sacred in oneself and in everything and everyone may seem far-fetched and unrealistic when seen from the perspective of horror filled acts which come to light in daily events the world over. The movie "Fargo," based on a true story taking place in Minnesota (the Luther land for some of us in the USA), the horrific slaughter of students and faculty bombings of the twin towers in New York on September 11, 2001 or the daily killings and maiming or injuring the creative essence of all things takes on new forms and life continues. Somehow, though, the destructive action of one can be attributed to an awareness that was never conveyed, or an awareness denied by concentration on the individual self apart from a conscious relationship to the whole. And for that we are all responsible.

The question then becomes, 'how do we convey or inculcate the awareness of the sacred within ourselves and others?"

Beyond Me.

I know that something inside my own disposition insists that I do my best to preserve whatever it is that is life or life giving in me. But I would never have the courage or lack of temerity to say of myself that I am sacred. Someone else might convey that notion to me, and I might lay hold of it however briefly for a time, but it would take repeated assurances of the same to sustain this attitude. And it would always have the companionship of considerable doubt. It could be a Mother, Dad, a beloved teacher, very gracious people along the way, a generous hand extended when I am down, a tilt in the direction of what is possible, even for me. Such people and such actions might serve to preserve the reserve otherwise wanting, not only in myself but in countless other people.

From time immemorial Jesus has been said to be divine. Nobody knows what that means. The only thing I can be sure of after years of study to discover what Jesus was about, is that he, in innumerable ways, was able to reach out to those who saw themselves far from the precincts called sacred.

They were, indeed, sacred in themselves. In that sense I believe that Jesus saw what was sacred in human beings—what it means to be truly human-no matter how far we are from making any claims to distinction in a religious sense. Life, in itself, is sacred. To look for it in the people and the earth that surrounds us is the only sanctuary truly worthy of support. The sacred surrounds us, fills us, moves us forward, perpetuates whatever possibility or future we may have. We are constantly in need of reassurance of our own worth, singly and, most importantly, together. Well never make it alone. The abundant life is life for everybody, not just me. No sacred precinct exists apart from that. "The earth is the Lord's and the fullness thereof. " is the only faith claim that stands the light of reason or science unless we mean by that that "the Lord" has nothing to do with reality as we know it.

Idolatrous Worship

I know of no one in our time who would think of worshipping at the foot of idols. Whether we frequent houses of worship or never enter such a place, of one thing we can be sure. We would never consciously contribute to the worship of figures purported to be or represent one whom we would call God.

But are we so sure we have escaped the temptation? Have our ideas of 'God' so shaped our thoughts and gestures in worship in a way that has captured us, binding us to notions which confine, limiting access to people whose lives have not been enclosed within the traditions familiar to us? Have the words with which we have been taught to picture 'God set a boundary to our imaginations? Have we presumed to dictate the terms of admission to the sphere of what is basic and true to life? Is there no room for doubt? No room for new insights and expressions? No sense of wonder in the face of mysteries which lie beyond every form of expression or explanation? Have we captured 'God' in creeds which presume to define and restrict? Has assent to verbal formulae excluded the possibility of wonder? Are the awesome depths of reality a thing of the past? I think not.

Perhaps we would be better served if adoration and worship were to challenge and perhaps eliminate every creedal formulation. Perhaps we should confess, whether or not we are religiously inclined, that there is no way to suggest, much less define, the sacred essence of which we are all a part.

A Sense of the Sacred. Christmas, '06

Yesterday was Sunday, the fourth Sunday of Advent, with the worship service governed by the ancient texts. And the sermon which could be summed up in the words, "We are still waiting. It's not Christmas yet." The Lutheran liturgy, as you might know, has gradually taken the shape of ancient rites, often utilizing the metaphysical wording of the Nicene Creed, written to conform not only the practices of congregational worship in various locales, but also to please the political aspects of an empire intent upon extending its uniform understanding of elements which otherwise could be divisive to its interests.

I became aware of a tendency, common to us all, of directing our attention and devotion to the praise and glory of God away from our affirmation and uplifting of the plight of the earth, and of our fellow human beings. God (if we choose to use the name) or the creative thrust behind the universe of life, in things and in people, has no need of praise and glory. The wonder of it is continually revealed through science. Beyond all present measure, the notion of a creative force creates an awareness of a mystery which should lead everyone to a sense of awe. We had best look to the earth and, more especially, to the unique features of particular things and people whose potential genius might impart to us gifts of nature yet to be explored.

Have we been captured and enclosed in the limitations of the past, its formulations, perspectives and attitudes? Might we better search for the direction that might have been lost in the movement of life ages past when traditions ascribed to point an arrow to the future have taken to make claims upon truth as forever fixed rather than as an evolving continuing event?

I am reminded of a paragraph in Charles Frazier's novel THIRTEEN MOONS, words of Will, a boy bound to run a remote Indian trading post in frontiers yet unmapped. His adoptive father is Bear, a Cherokee chief. "I cannot decide whether it is an illness or a sin, to write things down and fix the flowing world in one rigid form. Bear believed writing dulled the spirit, stilled holy breath. Smothered it. Words, when they've been captured and imprisoned on paper, become against the world, one best left alone. Everything that happens is fluid, changeable. After they've passed, events are only as your memory makes them, and the shift shapes. Writing things down fixes it in place as surely as a rattlesnake skin stripped from the meat and stretched and tacked to a barn wall. Every bit as stationary, and every bit as false to the original thing. Flat and still and harmless. Bear recognized that all writing memorializes a momentary line of thought as if it were final."

I believe in the God who is over all, who is just, compassionate and merciful, actively creative, the source of wisdom and strength, comfort and guidance, for all who are attentive to sacred gift of life. I believe in the spirit embodied in Jesus of Nazareth who, by his life and teachings, brought healing, understanding and life to those who

sought grace and meaning for themselves
and for others in a community which is open
and affirming of that which is creative and
good.

I believe in the spirit, reflected throughout
the world in the lives and teachings of those
who have given themselves in the service
and enlightenment of others, now and in
ages past. I look for guidance of the spirit in
recognition of our interdependence and
mutual responsibility for the earth and one
another. Together may we seek justice,
express kindness and walk humbly before
our God.

I like to remember the sacred in all others
and in all things. Faith is to be lived. A
profession means nothing without the deeds
of service that go with it, including justice,
kindness and humility. We all need each
other, whether we admit it or not. We do
immeasurable harm to ourselves when we
think of ourselves as superior, further
advanced or special in comparison to others.

Sense of the Sacred. Living Our Faith.

I had a friend in New York, a classmate in grad school, who had served several terms as an army chaplain. Both of us were returning to academia with a view to enriching our preparations for ministry. There were two parishes of people whose families had come from Denmark. Both were in Brooklyn, one coming out of the traditions of the great pastor, teacher and author of many of Denmark's most loved hymns, N. F. S. Grundig. He was the founder of the folk schools of Denmark, emphasizing a broad educational background in all the arts. That local congregation had sent a team to the New York World's Fair folk dancing exhibition. The other was of the "Inner Mission." a very proper, some would say pietistic (if not legalistic) view of life to be lived in community. Both happened to need pastors, and both were ready to support persons like ourselves, ordained but presently carrying a heavy load of course work and research. He chose to serve the "Holy Danes," as we sometimes called them, because they had a large parsonage for his growing family. We were already situated in student housing at Union Theological Seminary and Columbia

University. Both of us were pleased to find a way to serve part time, thereby able to provide for needs of those congregations and for our own families.

Viggo Aronsen had a saying he did not mind uttering whenever someone addressed him as "Reverend." "Call me mister, call me friend, but do not call me reverend." I had always shared the same thought. No pastor is deserving of greater reverence than others in his flock, or in public. He is made of the "same stuff," warts and all. If he is doing his job he deserves respect, but so also do all those who support the programs of institutions serving people, and, as you may detect by time, my own inclination is to seek to remember the sacred in all others and in all things. Faith is to be lived. A profession means nothing without the deeds of service that go with it, including justice, kindness and humility. We all need each other, whether we admit it or not. We do immeasurable harm to ourselves when we think of ourselves as superior, further advanced or special in comparison to others.

Viggo and his family demonstrated that to us when we, a year later, having just moved into the redecorated and refurbished home of the "Happy Danes, the "Dancing Danes," caught fire due to a faulty connection between the furnace and the chimney. They came to us immediately and took us into their abode for the six or more weeks it would take to restore our new home. The message they delivered was encapsulate in the way they lived. Not only did they serve us, but they gave our children, and theirs, a delightful time together in what was a comparatively new setting for all of us.

What Do We Do with Jesus?

Having been thoroughly immersed the confessional scripts of the Lutheran Church, ordained, a parish pastor, holding a Ph- D. theology from New York's Union Theological Seminary with major attention to Biblical languages and literature, I could not, as a tenured professor of one of our seminaries, remain silent on question of what is meant by the claim that Jesus is divine, unique son of God, whose origin and presence is in the heavenly domain.

The traditional response, of course, is an appeal to the earliest writing as to the nature and life of Jesus, found in Paul's letter to the Philippians 2.5-11, the so-called Christ Hymn.
"Let the same mind be in you that was in Christ Jesus, who, though he was in the form (image. likeness) of God, did count equality with God as something to be exploited (grasped), but emptied himself, taking the form of a slave, being born in human likeness.
And found in human form, humbled himself and became obedient to the point of death—

even death on a cross. Therefore, also he was highly exalted and to him was given the name that is above every name, so that at the name of Jesus every knee should bend, in heaven and on earth and under the earth, and every tongue should confess that Jesus Christ is the son, to the glory of God the Father."

The traditional interpretation of that passage involves an act of Jesus descending from his abode in heaven to the earth, assuming human form, living, dying and then elevated to former estate to reign in the name of God. It was to this verse I turned in the second of two lectures given to a group of some three hundred pastors of the Minnesota Lutheran Church of America in the mid-sixties on the assigned subject of what was then known as the New Hermeneutics.

It seemed very clear to think, given Paul's references to the first Adam in the creation narratives of Genesis, he was simply seeing Jesus as Adam, "first of a new creation" (see Roman 8.29), a new generation. To me Paul was simply saying that Jesus had lived as the human has been given to live. He was what

God had intended for us all—to be human, given a place in the earth with authority (today we call it "consciousness") and responsibility over in all its forms. Today we could say that Jesus was aware of himself as part and parcel of the creative activity of God (the "void", the "vacuum", some would say), and that our task was to follow in his footsteps, to have the same mentality, the same consciousness of who we are meant to be. We are to be of the "same mind," conscious of ourselves as part of the creative activity in life.

There was a standing ovation from those in attendance. Unfortunately, some who were not there and some who considered themselves the authorities in the creedal and power structures of the Church were terribly disturbed that I should take seriously the claim

Jesus was a human being, a man, in likeness with us all. The implication, they felt, was a denial of his divinity.

What I had to ask, in response, was, "What do we mean by divinity? How are we able to describe or God? Today I would have to say that what we urgently need to see is that life, in all its forms, is sacred, and if we would wish to see or to know anything of what "God" is about we will have to be content with being attentive to all the things and persons who surround us and are part and parcel of what we ourselves are all about. Faith which is attentive will pay close attention to the development of an understanding and a perspective that takes seriously our role as responsible subjects in the world of which we are a part.

The implication, of course, is that every other claim from the earliest sources of the Christian tradition concerning the Jesus they had known contained within itself a message of importance to everyone. We should know ourselves as children of God, as unique, one of a kind element in the structure and form of living which is creative, vital, nourishing, liberating and affirming of ourselves within the mainstreams of life. And this without presumption that we have attained our potentials, having arrived at our final destiny that is open before us. We have a road to travel-- a path to follow. We are simply free to become all that we are possibly meant to be.

Orthodox Denial of Reality.

When we have been taught to respect our elders, when elders have selected leaders of whom it is said they are highly trained, extremely able and generally noted as authorities, the seeker, who is struggling for understanding, finds it difficult to contradict or even question what he is told. I would tend to agree that in my own search I have found it very difficult, at times even preposterous, to challenge "the truth" presented with such confidence and public support by those placed in positions of authority in churches and in the political domain. Most of us would like to think that what we believe and how we behave and give expression to life has the support of people recognized as competent. But the longer I live, the more I am convinced that the thing we should try to do in our search for understanding is to stop asking questions and, if sincerity is at the base of such questions, we need to be constantly open to reality. Though I have not always asked right questions I have become more and more open. To be open is to free, and to be free is to be responsible, and to be responsible is to be honest about where we stand and how we see with respect to the realities of life.

Orthodoxy is, by its very nature, a closed system. As such it is, of necessity, closed to reality from any point of view apart from its own. The world of such reality is a closed system, impenetrable, demanding recognition of authority which lies outside oneself. Beyond that system, that closed perspective, all else is labeled false, questionable, a challenge to whatever system or structure established to preserve, defend, or propagate the same.

So, typical of any child or youth living in an environment where respect for elders is normal, I was drawn to search among those whose groups encouraged godliness for some hint of a direction which pointed the way to tranquil and responsible living. My mother, considered as good and as godly as anyone I knew, was responsible for herself and for those with whom she came in contact. It was not because they were affiliated with any church, though nominally they were Lutherans, raised and confirmed as such in the Church of Norway, but because that was a way that all should know. Somewhere down the line of childhood toward becoming a youth, I realized more and more that within any society, there ought to be a way by which that could be eradicated among others who were not part of our family. I was concerned about myself among friends and acquaintances that pointed in a direction harmful to the personal and potential development we shared as a community. Friends whom I greatly admired and who were taking risks in behavior which, quite obviously, were good neither for themselves or for others. How could there be provided some corrective to that tendency which is present in everyone. Our personal identity must be nurtured apart from identity within a group. How can we create a community that preserves and enhances the best in each of us?

1 looked to the church to provide some means whereby I might find a stronger and more positive outlook and I sought to discover something of the disposition, knowledge, and abilities that would sustain hope for myself and for others. Little did I realize the breadth of understanding outside my own little world that would someday be opened before, but I did the best that I could to explore the depths of a world view that

dominates and enfolds so many in our culture. Christianity, by centuries of development under dedicated people, required much effort of anyone claiming a rigorous pursuit of the formative factors of that religious outlook. Little did I realize how deeply entrenched 1 could become, and with me thousands of others, in an outlook which could result in creating an understanding which excludes realities of life that is unfolding in directions far removed from the limiting strictures of our own particular society and the traditions we hold dear.

Traditions originally intended to give direction may be sterilized when remaining open is no longer an option; when dogma, repetitive ritualization, in thought and practice, leave no room for a greater world.

FAITH FOR TODAY

Genius from Other Lands.

It has been our distinct privilege to have experienced life in many parts of the world. west to east, north to south, residents during time in eleven of our states, six different countries on four continents, and having visited some thirty nations around the world, our lives have been enriched with every such move or visit. New vistas of understanding, broader bases for learning and greater appreciation of cultures, conditions and life-styles beyond the horizons of our own particular background are great treasure troves from which we constantly draw, whether consciously or otherwise. We have not been able to explore the depths of those treasures, of course, but they have served to keep us open and humble in the face of so much there is yet to learn. The industry, the scholarship, the art, the social fabric the character and the geographic conditions of life in all those places remind us, again and again, of our mutual needs, our common dependence and our composite future as a world in which, like it or not, we are one with all others.

Each of those places, openings for wonder, is represented in our minds, of course, by the faces of people we have met who, in themselves, have garnished the best from the garden of their own background, fertilizing our own with nutrients that promise growth. Growth in knowledge, in wisdom, in appreciation, in inspiration and productivity is beneficial for life, intellectually, physically and spiritually. There can be no real separation of life into compartments, of course, but there is a sense in which we discover that who others are, and whatever their unique characteristics might be, we have the privilege of being mutually enriched by every contact. We need one another.

Whatever genius we bring, however little that might be, is more than matched by the genius inherent to every region of this world, by the cultures those regions contain and by the people who have absorbed and been willing to share the genius of that culture with us. We can only be humble in the light of all that we have received on this journey that has been ours.

Norman K Bakken

<u>A Long Way to Go</u>.

The sacred is present within everything and everyone. Recognition of the same has a long way to go. There are a few people I have known in whom I could recognize none of that. Mainly because I knew so little of or about them. Our first pup, Pal, was half Collie and half English Shepherd. He was a beautiful dog. Auburn with white trim around his neck and on his paws. He was our great friend. The name tells you that. But you never touched his tail. If you came close to doing that you would hear an immediate growl Why? "Old Man Munson, the breeder, had the habit of swinging his pups by the tail. A beastly thing to do, we boys thought, and we, in turn, had the beastly thought that we would like to burn down his barn!

Many others, all kinds of people, we meet with every day; when we come to know them well we invariably find features we can admire, features we would love to claim as our own. But sometimes, we will discover elements falling far short of the label sacred. The trouble caused by such recognition, again almost invariably, comes from the fact that we do not know one another well enough. We have no idea how that trait found its place in that person. And he cannot imagine where we are coming from. So, we are placed in a position of opposition. Without compromise of some sort we simply part ways. Some of my saddest experiences have come from the sense of alienation which invariably comes with distrust we feel toward one another. There is a sense of war, a split, a divide opened between us. The option of mutual encouragement and support is blocked. So, we are robbed of the nourishment we might have derived from one another.

So, what are the options? We should keep looking, keep alert, remain attentive, so that there might be some way of opening a channel for the sacred we know is there, sacred which is life giving once it is recognized and given a place within our own identity. The power of one can be tremendous, but it takes the power of two to bring to pass the next stage in our development as human beings, Life at its best enfolds a meeting of opposites. The future is open for those who can embrace as their own those who are so different and therefore so essential to broadening our own horizons of possibility of the Idolatrous

Worship. I know of no one in our time who would think of worshipping at the foot of idols. Whether we frequent houses of worship or never enter such a place, of one thing we can be sure. We would never consciously accept worship of figures purported to be or represent one whom we would call God.

But are we so sure we have escaped the temptation? Have our ideas of 'God' so shaped our thoughts and gestures in worship in a way that has captured us, binding us to notions which confine, limiting access to people whose lives have not been enclosed within the traditions familiar to us? Have the words with which we have been taught to picture 'God' set a boundary to our imaginations? Have we presumed to dictate the terms of admission to the sphere of what is basic and true to life? Is there no room for doubt? No room for new insights and expressions? Have we captured God' in creeds which presume to define and restrict? Has assent to verbal formulae excluded the possibility of wonder? Are the awesome depths of reality a thing of the past? I think not.

Perhaps we would be better served if adoration and worship were to challenge and perhaps eliminate every creedal formulation. Perhaps we should confess, whether we are religiously inclined, that there is no way to suggest, much less define, the sacred essence of which we are all a part. Or is that confession, in and of itself, presumptuous?

Life, this life, is a treasure. Today, this day, we have life.

The only life worth living, and the only day worth sharing, is the one we give.

Is my life conditional? Does it depend on what I believe? Well, that depends on what we mean by believing.

Do I believe in God?

Yes. I believe in the creative impulse of the whole universe, the source of life, the giver of life, life in all its forms. I cannot imagine or describe 'God*' I am unable to explain what lies at the basis of life. itself, life in any form. As a theologian I must say that my task is to give expression to the inexpressible. As a scientist I would have to confess that we do not know the ultimate source of being, either in terms of matter or in terms of energy. Both the theologian and the scientist must remain humble, by the very nature of their discipline.

Do I believe in Jesus?

Yes. I believe in Jesus as the reflection of a life that is self- forgiving, self-surrendering, because he found his life in giving life to others. In that sense, for me, he reflects what life is all about, what might give meaning and direction, hope for the future, our future, in this life and on this earth. No one has been able to completely disclose the essence of what Jesus said and did. We know some of what we might call historical facts, but more than that we cannot say with certainty or completeness. The words we use to give expression to that faith are no match for the essence of his life or, for that matter, for the life of anyone who believes in him. His life is, in a sense, a part of every life he has touched, whether directly or indirectly, but, like life itself, his reflection of the essence of life is beyond imagination.

Jesus was unique, as is everyone—one of a kind. He is also part of us, part of our lives, as is everyone and everything. We are interrelated and interdependent, whether we know it or not and whether we can prove it or not. A creative life contributes to the life of every other. Nature has a way of utilizing our lives as a means of life that continues, perhaps in different forms.

Do I believe in the Spirit?
Yes. I believe that the source of life, awakened by the impulse of a life that is self-forgiving, based on the impulse of love, acts of compassion, and the desire to move

us forward in the realization of life in all its fullness. It is life that matters, life which is ours together, interrelated and interdependent as we are.

Altogether, what does that imply? What is my attitude toward others, toward the earth, toward the universal?

It means that I believe in life, in all its forms, from the tiniest creatures on earth, to the finest particles of life that make up the universe, to the most wonderful formations of stars and planets, lands and seas—all of which are a part of the life that has been given to us, which we may sense all around and within us. And that means that I believe in you, for I see in you a creative part of life itself, and I know that I am dependent on you, as we all are on one another, for life to continue. You, as you are, unique and sacred are a part of my life. That means, for me, that life and hope are produced at base by the energies at work through the love and compassion we can express, energies absolutely necessary for survival in any form. Apart from a life that is given, there is no life.

ABOUT THE AUTHOR

Norman K. Bakken, a retired minister of the Lutheran Church in America, has served pastorates in Seattle and New York City, prior to thirty years as a professor at seminaries and universities in the United States, Brazil, Jamaica, Indonesia, Tanzania, and India. He holds a B.A. from Augsburg College, and a M.Div. from Luther Theological Seminary. He has a PHD from Union Theological Seminary. He was honored with several research grants and teaching awards, including an Outstanding Educators of America Citation.

His home town is Everett, Washington, where he met his lifelong companion, Virginia Vigue Bakken (Ginger). Together they raised four children, Minda, Mark, Mary, and John. Through them they are now the proud grandparents of Marija and Tiana, children of Peter Ozolins and Mary Bakken, and Mateo, son of John and Liza Wenacur Bakken. Ginger died in 2012. Norman resides At Brandon Oaks Retirement Center in Roanoke, Virginia, where he is a leading light on matters of spirituality.

ISBN: 978-0-9978248-6-6

Brush Fork Press LLC
Miami, Florida
A Delaware Company

FAITH FOR TODAY

FAITH FOR TODAY

FAITH FOR TODAY

FAITH FOR TODAY

FAITH FOR TODAY

www.ingramcontent.com/pod-product-compliance
Lightning Source LLC
Chambersburg PA
CBHW060713030426
42337CB00017B/2857